The Fragrance
of
the Bride

Rebecca Park Totilo

The Fragrance of the Bride

Printed in the United States of America.

Cover Design by Rebecca Park Totilo

About the Cover: In ancient Israel and the Middle Eastern, the bride "stained" her hands and feet with Henna, symbolic of the bride price and ransom paid by the bridegroom. This bride's hand is elaborately decorated using Henna for her wedding.

Front Cover: Henna Bride Photo Copyright © 2008 Shannon Varis (iStockphoto.com). All rights reserved.

Back Cover: Pink Petal Photo Copyright © 2008 David Nicolas (Fotolia.com). All rights reserved.

Published by Rebecca at the Well Foundation, PO Box 60044, St. Petersburg, Florida 33784.

Scripture references are taken from the King James Version of the Bible.

ISBN 978-0-9749115-2-6

Table of Contents

A Fragrant Garden

And God said, Let the earth bring forth grass, the herb yielding seed, [and] the fruit tree yielding fruit after his kind, whose seed [is] in itself, upon the earth: and is was so.

— Genesis 1:11

When God created the earth, on the third day He made plants to produce leaves, blossoms, and fruits at certain times of the year (seasons). God designed our heart to grow like a garden—to bear herbs (leaves as beauty), flowers (blossoms emit a fragrance), and fruit (food offers

nourishment) according to the spiritual maturity we cultivate in our relationship with Him. These three reflect our character in the Messiah because they all reflect the loveliness and aroma of His character.

In the Old Testament, when the question of who would be the priests unto the Lord arose, Moses placed each of the staffs from the twelve tribes of Israel into the Ark of the Covenant overnight. Numbers 17:6-8 tells us Aaron's rod for the tribe of Levi "was budded, and brought forth buds, and bloomed blossoms, and yielded almonds."

As a partaker of the New Covenant, the Messiah's bride is called a "royal priesthood" unto Him. It is His priestly remnant who will carry out His plan by sharing in the priestly duties under our High Priest, Yeshua Ha Mashiach. His Temple (the body of Christ) needs caretakers to nurture and tend to the Lord's garden, in order to prepare for His return.

Think of how the thorn-less "Rose of Sharon" beautifully mirrors His tender love, as spoken of in Song of Solomon 2:1-2: "I [am] the rose of Sharon, and the lily of the valleys. As the lily among thorns, so [is] my love among the daughters."

As you read on, you will see a believer's life is not yet without thorns and in need of the Master Gardener's touch. We are to be "fruit examiners" and help those who are young and tender in the Lord to grow up and mature. Just as the master gardener would not tear his plants out of the ground before they have had the chance to bear fruit, a believer must not be critical of a new or immature believer, tending to God's garden in a judgmental way.

Song of Solomon chapter 7 tells how the bride and her beloved go out together to check the vineyards. In verses 11 and 12, the bride says to her beloved shepherd (representing Yeshua), "Come, my beloved, let us go forth into the field... Let us get up early to the vineyards; let us see if the vine flourish, [whether] the tender grape appear, [and] the pomegranates bud forth."

The Lord and His beloved pictured here are working together, being attentive to the signs of new spiritual growth and fruit in her life and in the lives of others wherever they go.

Together with the Messiah, we must go out and inspect our own vineyard for character growth and maturity (not necessarily for fruit—trees and vineyards bear fruit in its season), but to make sure it is kept in order so that we will bear fruit.

Song of Solomon 4:13-14 list the contents of His betrothed's garden:

> Thy plants [are] an orchard of pomegranates, with pleasant fruits; camphire, with spikenard, spikenard and saffron; calamus and cinnamon, with all trees of frankincense; myrrh and aloes, with all the chief spices.

In this short study, we will be looking at this bouquet of fragrances that make us the "sweet savour of Christ" (2 Corinthians 2:15).

Myrrh

A bundle of myrrh [is] my well-beloved
unto me; he shall lie all night between my
breasts.

— Song of Solomon 1:13

Fragrances and herbs mentioned in the Holy Scriptures are physically enriching as well as rich spiritually with
symbolism. Each represents the virtues and characteristics
of Yeshua's perfection and what He desires in the Bride of
Messiah.

Myrrh

We see the revelation of spices and fragrances in Song of Solomon 1:13. In the bride's response to the King, her statement reflects a popular custom of laying a bundle of myrrh on one's chest while sleeping as a beauty treatment in preparation for a wedding.

The Hebrew word for myrrh is *Mowr* which means "distilled," and comes from the root word *Marar* which means "bitterness."

During the Messiah's final agonizing hours in the Garden of Gethsemane, the weight of the world's sins crushed our Savior like a wine press, causing Him to sweat great tears of blood. His bitter sufferings can be compared to myrrh, a highly-prized spice used for perfumes and incense, extracted by piercing the tree's heartwood and allowing the gum to trickle out and harden into bitter, aromatic red droplets called "tears." When the myrrh flows from the tree, it is distilled in bitterness.

As joint heirs with the Messiah, we are to share in His afflictions according to 2 Corinthians 1:5, so that we His bride can be triumphant through the bitterness of suffering.

Myrrh represents the bitter sufferings of Yeshua as a man on earth, whereby He learned obedience unto death by emptying himself of His own will (Hebrews 5:8; Philippians 2:7-8).

As His bride, just as the disciples did, we must follow Yeshua in denying one's own will so as to obey Him (Matthew 16:24-25).

Myrrh signifies the bitter sufferings of Yeshua at Calvary. The Scriptures says in Isaiah 53:5, "But he [was] wounded for our transgressions, [he was] bruised for our iniquities."

In the book of Esther we learn how Hadassah (Esther's Hebrew name, which means "myrtle") underwent almost a year of beauty treatments with spices and cosmetics to make her desirable for the King. Esther was prepared with the help of a eunuch (symbolic of the Holy Spirit) that provided her with the oil of myrrh. In the way Esther was prepared, the Spirit provides His betrothed with the oil of myrrh which allows us to share in His sufferings. Philippians 3:10-11 tells us:

That I may know him, and the power of his resurrection, and the fellowship of his sufferings, being made conformable unto his death; if by any means I might attain unto the resurrection of the dead.

The Scriptures also tell us to rejoice in these trials. Colossians 1:24 says, "Who now rejoice in my sufferings for you, and fill up that which is behind on the afflictions of Christ in my flesh for his body's sake, which is the church."

As part of the body of Messiah, we too will bear His portion of affliction, as a part of Him. However, since the bride is considered the "second Eve," like her we have been taken out of the side of the "last Adam" and will be taken to a place of protection during the final hours of Jacob's trouble.

In fact, when the Messiah returns for His bride, we will actually "smell" His coming because His garments have been soaked in these fragrances in the midst of the throne room. Revelation 8:3-4 tells us that the original altar of incense continues to be used before the throne of God in

Heaven. Psalm 45:8 describes Yeshua's garments: "All thy garments [smell] of myrrh, and aloes, [and] cassia, out of the ivory palaces, whereby they have made thee glad."

These spices are emitted in our lives when we clothe ourselves with righteous acts and deeds as the Bride of Christ and spend quality time with Him. Just like when a spouse or good friend greets you with a hug and is wearing cologne or perfume, their fragrance lingers with you after they are gone. So it is with Yeshua. People will begin to recognize there is something different about you when you have been in His presence. Hebrews 1:8-9 affirms that this Psalm refers to the marriage of Yeshua.

In the next chapter, we will continue to study the other spices that make up the formula of the "fragrance of Christ to our Heavenly Father" as mentioned in the Old Testament and again in 2 Corinthians 2:15: "For we are unto God a sweet savour of Christ, in them that are saved, and in them that perish."

Cassia

And of cassia five hundred [shekels], after
the shekel of the sanctuary, and of oil olive a
hin.

— Exodus 30:24

Cassia, considered an inferior plant to the other species in the laurel family, is mentioned in the book of Exodus
as part of the holy anointing oil. The Hebrew word for
"cassia" is *Qiddah*, which is similar to the word meaning "to
bow down" or "to pay homage." "Homage" in Scripture
means to honor another by bending low in deep respect.

Yeshua said, "I honor My Father... I seek not mine own glory" in John 8:49-50.

Like cassia, Yeshua was considered lowly and honored the Father in everything He did. The leaders considered Him of little account because He came from Nazareth, but His Father glorified Him as mentioned in John 8:54: "Jesus answered, If I honor myself, my honor is nothing: it is my Father that honoreth me; of whom ye say, that he is your God."

As His bride, we are to be humble toward all people. And, as Yeshua, we are to bow down in homage to the Heavenly Father alone.

Aloes

I have perfumed my bed with myrrh, aloes,
and cinnamon.

— Proverbs 7:17

There are two plants referred to as "aloes" in the Bible. One is a rich, fragrant resin formed in the heartwood of the aquilaria tree, in response to a natural parasite, fungal, or mold attack. Burying the logs, the outer part decays while the inner, saturates with this resin. The tree may also be deliberately wounded to make it susceptible to attack. Thus, the fungus and decomposition process can take over several hundred years to produce, making it one of the most rare and expensive oils. The wounding of the "heartwood" of the tree

In Isaiah 53:5, Isaiah prophesied of the Messiah's crucifixion, saying, "But he [was] wounded for our transgressions, [he was] bruised for our iniquities: the chastisement of our peace [was] upon him; and with his stripes we are healed."

Deliberately wounded for our disobedience of the law, Yeshua took our punishment so that we could be reconciled to God and walk again in the fullness of God.

The second is "lign aloes" mentioned in Balaam's blessing for Israel. Numbers 24:6 says, "As the valleys are they spread forth, as gardens by the river's side, as the trees of lign aloes which the LORD hath planted, [and] as cedar trees beside the waters."

The Arabic word for "aloes" in this verse means "little tents," derived from the triangular shape of the capsules from the lign aloes trees, and its resin emits this fragrant spice. These "little tents" refer to a tent on the housetop—a place of intimacy or bridal tent. It was a common practice in the Middle East to build a small "honeymoon suite" on the rooftop of a house. 2 Samuel 16:22 tells how they "spread a tent on the top of the house" for Absalom.

After the betrothal ceremony in ancient Israel, the bridegroom left the bride's home and returned to his father's house to prepare for his wedding day. Before departing, he made a special promise to his bride: "I go and prepare a place for you and when it is ready, I will return for you." During this time of separation, the groom built a bridal chamber or tent attached to his father's house, while the bride gathered her trousseau and made herself ready for his return.

Like an Israeli bridegroom, Yeshua comforts His disciples with these same words before He returns to His Father's house, spoken in the ancient Jewish rite in John 14:1-2: "Let not your heart be troubled... In my Father's house are many mansions: if [it were] not [so], I would have told you. I go to prepare a place for you."

He reaffirms His followers that He will come to sequester us into the bridal tent He has made ready for His bride.

Calamus

Dan also and Javan going to and fro occupied in thy fairs: bright iron, cassia, and calamus, were in thy market.

— Ezekiel 27:19

Calamus is mentioned in Exodus 34 as part of the Exodus anointing oil as well as a principle chief spice in Song of Solomon and Ezekiel. The word "calamus" in Hebrew is *Qaneh*, which means "a stalk or aromatic reed." It is translated as "right or upright, balances and measuring rod" in Scripture.

The first biblical example of the word to mean "moral uprightness" was God saying, "Do that which is right in his sight" in Exodus 15:26.

Yeshua alone is upright and righteous in His Father's eyes. 2 Corinthians 5:21 tells us: "For he hath made him [to be] sin for us, who knew no sin; that we might be made the righteousness of God in him."

The Scriptures tell us Yahweh searches to and fro for those who are upright. 2 Chronicles 16:9 says:

> For the eyes of the LORD run to and fro throughout the whole earth, to show himself strong in the behalf of [them] whose heart [is] perfect toward him. Herein thou hast done foolishly: therefore from henceforth thou shalt have wars.

In both Hebrew and Arabic, the root word *Kiddah* signifies "a strip," referring to the strips of bark from which the spice is made. In addition to being "upright" in God's eyes, cassia spiritually speaks of being stripped of arrogance and pride and walking in humility with a servant's heart and attitude. This is also one of the fragrances mentioned in Psalm 45:8 that Yeshua garments are soaked in.

Cinnamon

I have perfumed my bed with myrrh, aloes, and cinnamon.

— Proverbs 7:17

The primary root of the word "cinnamon" means "emitting an odor," while spiritually it speaks of holiness and set-apartness. In the Song of Solomon, cinnamon grows in a locked garden that Yeshua calls "my sister, [my] spouse" (Song of Solomon 4:12-14).

For every new believer, the heart is a fragrant garden, enclosed and set apart for Him alone. We must allow the Father to form and shape us into the image of Him and share the heart of the Lord that is undivided in devotion to Him.

Thanks be to God, who always leads us triumphant in Christ, and manifests through us the sweet aroma of the knowledge of Him in every place. For we are a fragrance of Christ to God (2 Corinthians 2:14-15).

Spikenard

Then took Mary a pound of ointment of spikenard, very costly, and anointed the feet of Jesus, and wiped his feet with her hair: and the house was filled with the odor of the ointment.

— John 12:3

Spikenard is a costly spice which comes from a very rare plant and is usually blended with olive oil for anointing acts of consecration, dedication, and worship.

Spikenard

The word "spikenard" in Hebrew is *Nard* and means "light." Interestingly, the message delivered in 1 John 1:5 talks about the nature of the Father, who is visible in Heaven by the pure, uncreated light of His nature. Yeshua Himself shared in this glory at the Mount of Transfiguration when the divine light was visible as He transfigured in a whiteness which was beyond any earthly whiteness as described in Mark 9:3. Soon, His bride will share in this glorious apparel as our wedding garments, mentioned in the book of Revelation. Revelation 19:8 says: "And to her was granted that she should be arrayed in fine linen, clean and white: for the fine linen is the righteousness of saints."

In Greek, the word for "spikenard" means "genuine and pure." In John 12:3, the Bible tells how spikenard was used to anoint Yeshua, the pure and spotless Lamb, just days before His death and burial:

> Then Mary took a pound of ointment of spikenard, very costly, and anointed the feet of Jesus, and wiped his feet with her hair: and the house was filled with the odor of the ointment.

Mark 14:3 tells us of another woman who came, having an alabaster flask of very precious oil of spikenard. After she broke the seal and poured the oil on Yeshua's head, some of the disciples were very indignant with the "waste" of costly oil, as it may have cost this woman as much as a whole year's wages. But Yeshua rebuked them and said she had done a good work, for He knew His life would soon be broken, just like the alabaster jar filled with the costly scent. Not a drop of her extravagant act of worship was wasted in His eyes. Yeshua said her deed would be remembered wherever the Gospel would be preached.

Whisper words of adoration, shout praises to His name—for every silent bowed knee or shout from the hilltop reaches His throne. Worship extravagantly! God doesn't see it as a waste and the Messiah won't leave us alone to "waste away" either. Instead, the oil—symbolic of the inner working of the *Ruach Ha Kodesh*—has been poured out for us, so we can live a life that is rich with a sweet, heavenly fragrance. As believers, we must worship Him with a pure, genuine heart of devotion and worship.

Solomon prophesied a thousand years earlier of this momentous event. Song of Solomon 1:12 says, "While the king [sitteth] at his table, my spikenard sendeth forth the smell thereof."

In this verse, the King is sitting, which is symbolic of His finished work at Calvary's tree. He is inviting her to come and join Him at the marriage supper feast. The bride's fragrance emanates out of her spirit in worship and adoration for the King's provision. This is a heavenly fragrance we should all possess.

Henna

My beloved is to me a cluster of camphire
in the vineyards of En-gedi.

— Song of Solomon 1:14

The Hebrew word for "camphire" (henna) means "a ransom," with its root word meaning "to forgive."

In the Middle East, a bride applies the spice of henna as a paste to her hands and feet on the night before her wedding. This spice yields a red stain which signifies the ransom of sinners who through the shedding of Yeshua's blood on the tree.

In Isaiah 43:3-4 it says:

For I [am] the LORD thy God, the Holy One of Israel, thy Savior: I gave Egypt [for] thy ransom, Ethiopia and Seba (Sheba) for thee. Since thou wast precious in my sight, thou hast been honorable, and I have loved thee: therefore will I give men for thee, and people for thy life.

Think for a moment about what the hands and feet of our Lord did for us. His were stained with blood for the forgiveness of sins and as a ransom for His bride.

For the believer, the hands signify work and the feet represent the way in which we walk. Our lives are to give forth the sweet fragrance of the Messiah's sacrifice on the tree as our ransom for sin.

1 Timothy 2:6 tells us: "Who gave himself a ransom for all, to be testified in due time."

The way we walk and behave toward all men and our acts of deeds and charity emits a fragrance for the world to savor. Ephesians 5:2 says, "And walk in love, as Christ also hath loved us, and hath given himself for us an offering and a sacrifice to God for a sweet smelling savor."

Ephesians 5:3-4 go on to say what is a stench in the nostrils of Yahweh:

> But fornication, and all uncleanness, or covetousness, let it not be once named among you, as becometh saints; neither filthiness, nor foolish talking, nor jesting, which are not convenient: but rather giving of thanks.

Through the triumph of the tree, Yeshua's resurrection gives us victory over the enemies of God (1 John 5:4; Hebrews 2:13). The bride price and ransom He paid was very costly and is represented by saffron, a most expensive spice.

Henna

In the Song of Solomon 4:12-14, Solomon responds to the Shulamite with these words:

> A garden enclosed [is] my sister, [my] spouse; a spring shut up, a fountain sealed. Thy plants [are] an orchard pomegranates, with pleasant fruits; camphire, with spikenard, spikenard and saffron; calamus and cinnamon, with all trees of frankincense; myrrh and aloes, with all the chief spices.

Our garden is a private garden with walls, for Him only. It is for His pleasure and His friends, the Heavenly Father, and the *Ruach Ha Kodesh* (Holy Spirit) to partake of our fruit, indicating the Messiah is being fruitful in our life.

The Shulamite continues in Song of Solomon 4:16:

> Awake, O north wind; and come, thou south; blow upon my garden, [that] the spices thereof may flow out. Let my beloved come into his garden, and eat his pleasant fruits.

The Fragrance of the Bride

The Shulamite bride cries out to Yah to blow upon her garden. She feels confident He will be with her regardless of any situation she will face. Whether the circumstances are harsh (north wind) or pleasant (south wind), the bride's heart will grow in maturity with her Beloved, emitting a fragrance from her soul.

Frankincense

And the LORD said unto Moses, Take unto
thee sweet spices, stacte, and onycha, and gal-
banum; [these] sweet spices with pure frankincense; of each shall there be a like [weight].

— Exodus 30:34

The Hebrew word "frankincense" means "pure or
white," because of the snowcapped mountains of Lebanon
where frankincense is grown, as well as the milk-colored
drops of aromatic resin that flow from the slashed inner
wood of the tree.

The Scriptures describe in Psalm 133:2 how Aaron was anointed with the Holy anointing oil (which included frankincense) for priestly service. It tells of how this oil dripped down upon his head, running down his beard to the edges of his robe, indicating that it was more than just a dab on the forehead!

Yeshua's priestly bride is anointed with the Holy Spirit, by our High Priest Yeshua, and should emanate from our wedding garments as well. Revelation 1:6 says: "And hath made us kings and priests unto God and his Father; to him [be] glory and dominion for ever and ever. Amen."

One of the priestly duties prescribed for the Levites as ministers of the Lord was to burn incense before the ark in the Holy of Holies. Exodus 30:8 tells us, "And when Aaron lighteth the lamps at even, he shall burn incense upon it, a perpetual incense before the LORD throughout your generations."

Frankincense, a main ingredient of this incense, burned day and night before Yahweh. This white pillar of smoke that ascended, reaching toward Heaven represented the prayers of the saints rising before His throne. The book of Revelation 5:8 says:

> And when he had taken the book, the four beasts and four [and] twenty elders fell down before the Lamb, having every one of them harps, and golden vials full of odors, which are the prayers of saints.

A portion of this prescribed incense was not burned but simply placed before the ark in the Holy of Holies. God said that this is "where I will meet with thee: it shall unto you most holy" (the holiest). Leviticus 24:7 says, "And thou shalt put pure frankincense upon [each] row, that it may be on the bread for a memorial, [even] an offering made by fire unto the LORD."

Pure frankincense was placed on the loaves of bread (representing Yeshua) to symbolize the purity and fragrance of Christ, the true bread of God. We are reminded of Yeshua's words in John 6:32: "Then Jesus said unto them, Verily, verily, I say unto you, Moses gave you not that bread from heaven; but my Father giveth you the true bread from heaven."

This portion represented the intercessory prayer made by Yeshua to God on our behalf, and He continues to pray for you.

Saffron

Spikenard and saffron; calamus and cinnamon, with all trees of frankincense; myrrh and aloes, with all the chief spices.

— Song of Solomon 4:14

Saffron is a very expensive spice from an orange-yellow flower of the crocus family. It is literally worth its weight in gold because it is the stigmas from which the spice is obtained. Each one is handpicked and placed over a charcoal fire for drying. It takes over 75,000 flowers to make one pound of saffron.

Saffron symbolizes the costly but triumphant faith of the Messiah against His enemy. Believers can live by faith just as the disciples did, knowing that the testing of their faith through fire will be more precious than gold. 1 Peter 1:7-8 says that:

> That the trial of your faith, being much more precious than of gold that perisheth, though it be tried with fire, might be found unto praise and honor and glory at the appearing of Jesus Christ: whom having not seen, ye love; in whom, though now ye see [him] not, yet believing, ye rejoice with joy unspeakable and full of glory.

Hebrews 11:6 tells us, "But without faith [it is] impossible to please [him]: for he that cometh to God must believe that he is, and [that] he is a rewarder of them that diligently seek him."

Allow the Lord to complete His perfect work in your character and place these beautiful fragrances in the garden of your heart.

Pomegranate

And [beneath] upon the hem of it thou shalt
make pomegranates [of] blue, and [of] purple,
and [of] scarlet, round about the hem thereof;
and bells of gold between them round about.

— Exodus 28:33

Highly esteemed by Israelites, the pomegranate was
believed to be the "original forbidden fruit" in the Garden of
Eden. It was also one of the seven species brought back by
the spies to show how fertile the Promised Land was.

Pomegranate

Carved figures of the pomegranate were principal ornaments adorning stately columns and pillars in Solomon's temple as well as worn on the High Priests garments symbolizing life.

The Hebrew word for "pomegranate" is *Ramam*, which means "to rise up" or "to be mounted up."

In Song of Solomon 4:3, Solomon describes his bride's "temples are like a piece of a pomegranate within thy locks."

Solomon uses the pomegranate theme for her temples to show fertility of the mind, where good seed is planted and a harvest is sure. Her thoughts are on what is pure, lovely, and of good report. She is the true bride, with the mental state that matches the King's. Here the Holy Spirit finds a welcome depository for "things that are to come."

Here the words of Yeshua are quickly brought to mind. She has the mind of Christ.

The pomegranate fruit, in relation to our temples, signifies that it is now the "fruit of the Spirit" that controls our lives (mounts or raises us up or above) rather than the lust of the flesh. The phrase "within thy locks" shows that she bears spiritual fruit that is veiled and hidden from the world for only the Lord to behold.

Some interpreters believe the reference to pomegranates is a symbol of fertility. On a holy theme, greater significance might point to the use of the pomegranate as it relates to the skirt of the high priest. At the bottom of the high priest's robe were pomegranates interspersed with bells. With every step, the ringing of bells with the symbol for "fertility of life" bore witness to sight and sound to declare life. Life and abundance characterizes the Savior's bride.

About Rebecca

Rebecca at the Well Foundation is a non-profit Judeo-Christian organization devoted to inspiring believers to prepare for the return of the Messiah. By informing the "called out ones" the way to walk in the beauty of holiness, it motivates members of the body to be clothed with righteous acts and deeds as the Bride of Messiah.

In an effort to bridge the gap between Judaism and Christianity, Rebecca at The Well Foundation provides workshops and seminars about the Hebraic roots of our faith that binds us together as one. All believers can celebrate Yeshua's return as they learn how to make themselves ready as a pure and holy bride.

Rebecca Park Totilo, founder and president of the Rebecca at The Well Foundation, is currently touring the country, preparing the bride for her Heavenly Bridegroom. She is available to speak at conferences, seminars and retreats. Please contact her at (727) 688-2115 for more information, or if you would like to have her come and share with your group or congregation.

Visit our website at: www.rebeccaatthewell.org

For e-mail correspondence:
becca@RebeccaAtTheWell.org

For snail mail correspondence:
Rebecca At The Well Foundation
PO Box 60044
St. Petersburg, FL 33784

Notes

Notes

CPSIA information can be obtained at www.ICGtesting.com
Printed in the USA
LVOW110009180512

282143LV00001B/28/P